The Only Voice I Could Hear Was Yours

Uzma Khan

Published by New Generation Publishing in 2018

Copyright © Uzma Khan 2018

First Edition

The author asserts the moral right under the Copyright, Designs and Patents Act 1988 to be identified as the author of this work.

All Rights reserved. No part of this publication may be reproduced, stored in a retrieval system or transmitted, in any form or by any means without the prior consent of the author, nor be otherwise circulated in any form of binding or cover other than that which it is published and without a similar condition being imposed on the subsequent purchaser.

www.newgeneration-publishing.com

Dedication

This book is dedicated to my sons Ibraheem and Shayaan. Thank you for being my source of strength, as you both continue to bring hope in my life.

To my family and friends for supporting me, thank you all for encouraging me to write, especially my brother Zuhaib and sister Zara.

Contents

Heart 1

Rooftop memories 2

A note to my mother 3

Broken home 4

Who am I 6

Time 7

Strength 8

Play of life 9

Pieces of mirror 10

Why did I love 11

A place I now despise 12

A love that only served you 13

A hypocrite world 14

Broken by your persona 15

Life's chaos 16

Conformity never ends 17

Seek within 18

Afraid to love 19

Lost in you 20

Fallen in love 21

I became a part of your world 22

Arranged marriage turned love 23

Affection 24

My love for you 25

Touch	26
A dream	27
Long distance	28
The star we saw	29
A memory	30
A part of me still wants you	31
A balm to my wounds	32
Intoxicate	33
I still think of you	34
I wonder	35
Escapism	36
Conscious and subconscious	37
Words	38
Voice	39
Lost heart	40
I wish I could fly away	41
Time	42
A matter of dignity	43
Replaced	44
A relationship	45
Years of Love	46
Love	47
Seven seas	49
I felt I found you	50
A promise unfulfilled	51

Your words 52

The moon 53

Blind faith 54

My heart 55

Your love was my foe 56

Under the stars 57

A lover or a liar 58

Not the man I loved 59

Promises 60

Unsteady hand 61

Carry on 62

Struggle with real emotions 63

Your love fooled me twice 64

Illusion of love 65

Presence and absence 66

Tough times 67

The other woman 68

The truth 69

Hatred and pain 70

Love not for me 72

Pain relief 73

Courage 74

9 months 75

Flowers 76

Divorce 77

Father 78
Lost it all 79
Your little face 80
Your name doesn't sting 81
Heavy heart 82
A poet 83
A lover now a stranger 84
Restless vs peaceful nights 85
Hardship 86
Broken pieces 87
Well being 88
Blessings change 89
Mindfulness 90
I love you my child 91
Healed by motherhood 92
A mother is never alone 93
Happiness 94
Loving yourself is still possible 95
Finding myself 96
Three words only 97
Peace in prayer 98
Prayer 99
Faith in yourself 100
Freedom 101
Time 102

Love or hate	103
Mistakes set me free	104
Definitions	105
Mother and a maid	106
A loyal star	107
The sky	108
The moon follows me	109
Solitude	110
My only reason why	111
I watch the world go by	112
Reminisce	113
The things we chase	114
Forget me not	115
My journey	116
Lines on your hands	117
Name fades	118
Single motherhood	119
The scars of life	124
Modesty in words	125
Stages of life	126

Heart

This heart I carry
is the biggest burden
on my soul
It clenches
and soaks up
everything I see
hear and touch

Rooftop memories

The sweltering heat, smothering humidity
I walk on the rooftop, reminiscing those years
They speak of tales, their secrets we hold
as each household tip toes, to come out to talk
The frayed delicate kites, lost and alone
trapped by their owner, as they pull back the roll
They search their way up, flying high and fearless
until it's cut by the sharpness, of a hidden eye.

As I look far ahead, through the clear hollow skies
the sound of the call, echoes the prayer for its time
The voice gently touches, unfamiliar parts of my soul
a sadness in its timbre, leaves a strange longing for more
A feeling of serenity, harmony and silence
the busy city slowly, comes to a hold
A place full of memories, scented with rose petals
a familiar attachment, I will never disown

A note to my mother

Growing up, you were my knight in shining armour
my protector, teacher, a shield in disguise
I loved you and still love you more than ever
even when things are not the same anymore

I closed my eyes, wherever you took me
my life, my soul, you shaped every corner
You took my hand, firmly by your side
'dive' you instructed, as I jumped right in
Drowning in water, as I tried to swim
you pulled me back, before I could think
lost in fear and afraid to speak

You took my hand, firmly by your side
following you in every direction you pulled
my life, my soul, you shaped every corner
you instructed a second time, I dove again deeper
Drowning with the waves, as I swept away further
you let go of my hand, unaware of what you did
I floated to the top, I learnt how to swim
I felt the water intensely, I feared it no more

I wanted to swim and took a dive once more
with no hand to hold, you left me on my own
when I called for you, you were already gone

Broken home

As my mother and father, both paint in symmetry
the colours splash together, on the canvas affectionately
A feeling of comfort, a place called home
somewhere I always felt really warm
One day I wondered, I will be like them
paint a symmetry in my own den

As the lines on my palm, differed from my mother's
my canvas was broken, with two specks of colours
Picking up my brush, with no symmetry in sight
I started writing, in the middle of the night
Fearlessly stubborn, I wiped away my tears
held myself together, with patience and prayers
Creating words of pain, as they flowed naturally
the pieces of canvas, I glued back myself
A feeling of confidence, faith and stability
I finally have a place I can call my home

Who am I

As I walk alone, in the midst of crowds
laughter, conversations, food they shout
Our happiness in others
our emotions they console
we hand ourselves, to others to control

I wonder is life a social necessity
Or a journey of unexplored self-discovery

I walk on the concrete, silent roads
they recognise my footsteps, my pitch, my tone
They remember me, know me as a part of them
Still and dead, as we walk over them

We come alone and we die alone
Yet we wonder, if we can live without another soul

Preserve yourself
Protect yourself
No one will ever know you more

Time

It was this time, last year
you came to my world
As I held you against my breast
I promised to raise you alone

It was this time, last year
you left me on my own
You threw me in your whirlwind
as I fought the storm on shore

It was this time, two years ago
I fell again for your words
each day I believed you
while you amused my soul

As the months passed by
I waited to see, how long,
I was able to survive this calamity
But I never knew, how wrong I was
when time and karma, always stood beside me

Strength

I never knew I had strength
lost in the bubble of naivety
Life always had a way with me
until I pushed each barrier firmly
I fought many battles within myself
suppressing each sorrow, beneath my skin
Coming this far and still holding on
the lioness in me, breaks the silence
once and for all

Play of life

I take off the masks, in the darkness of night
tired and exhausted, from the play of life
I try and find hope, in the small rays of light
looking at myself, from a different sight

My mask of a mother, dressed in flowers
loves and nurtures, its fluttering kites in all hours
My mask of a daughter, glazed in royal blue
reminds me of my responsibilities
and dues to my broken pool
My mask of a sister, stitched in shades of green
spreads harmony and security
to the seeds growing into trees

I gently dust the pieces,
of the mask of the woman inside
embellished in the colours
of black, gold and white
I look in the mirror, a reflection of a broken soul
a title, a status I proudly hold

Pieces of mirror

I look for myself
in the broken pieces of mirror
each reflection, speaks a story of my past
The glass pierces the tips of my fingers
as I pick them individually
remembering who I was

Why did I love

You gave me memories
from a place I fell in love with
which without you
would have felt incomplete

A place I now despise

I travelled to a place, far from where I lived
an arranged marriage, where my life begins
I began to see, through the windows of your eyes
as you gradually taught me, how to live
I felt a part of you, assured, who you were
A place I despise, now haunted by your words
each and every corner, walks your shadow and curse
Afraid to face the pieces, of those images left behind
a place I never want to see again, until the day I die

A love that only served you

I was lost in the mirage
of finding my happiness,
in the well of love you showed me
A love you defined
and carved for yourself
I was thoughtlessly
following

A hypocrite world

My innocence I miss so dearly
with the purity I once saw things
Relations are only a means
and love a concept we lose
mocked for our sincerities
the world runs on infidelity
Your views and opinions
suppressed by the one
who owns your authority
Hesitant to meet others
unable to see right through
If only I could change myself
to blend in with the rest of you

Broken by your persona

We are all broken mortals
with a string of trials and belongings
A heart that is numb, a cautious eye
an ear that listens, to the hidden lies
We have learnt to shield, the organs of our bodies
the effects of which, remain scarred on our souls

We think before we trust
We hold before we love
We prefer to be alone

Broken by your persona

Life's chaos

In the midst of life's chaos, we lose the person inside
so much to worry and live up to, with no one there to guide
Our search for self-identity, ends when we enter the world
Feeling guilty and insignificant, to find time for ourselves
Compromising for others, years of burdens to pay
living a life carelessly, a choice we never made

Conformity never ends

You've been listening to your parents
your peers and then to the person you love
The small voice inside you
now makes you feel afraid and vulnerable
All this time they've continually reminded you
your words and judgements
carry less weight than others
How will I ever know if my heart
and mind will guide me or abandon me
You leave me with no choice
as I helplessly surrender

Seek within

We chase and fulfil relations our whole life
with no guarantee they will last forever
Seek to build an attachment with yourself
ready to carry your broken soul
in the solitude they leave behind

Afraid to love

I always kept myself, in a world inside my head
Inexpressive, unaffectionate, my feelings I hid
Afraid to love, to let go and to get close
I kept myself away, from the stories I heard
I spoke a little less, I saw a lot less
my virtues I lost, following others that led
I held my heart tightly, in the grip of my hands
but you still managed to take it, charmingly

Lost in you

Whilst discovering myself
I lost my way and met you
Spending the rest of my life
writing about you

Fallen in love

As you whispered my name
with words scented in musk
It was then I had fallen in love

I became a part of your world

I showed you my world
you gave me a peek of yours
Gently taking my hand
I merged into your life

Arranged marriage turned love

I became your Mrs, a title you embraced me with
a feeling of hesitance, as I began to let you in
Your gaze spoke of eternity, your touch of warmth
you were gradually becoming my weakness and need
As I held the pen from you, signing myself away
a mystery and an attachment, your depth I felt so near
The chants you would sing, in declaration of your love
your essence I felt so pure
pulling me towards you, like a dove
First love, soul mate, you became everything, so fast
your notes, your care, a gift so precious
I kept it sacred, which was no easy task
My promise in return
I gave you the keys to my heart

Affection

The way your eyes speak to me
a flush of heat, rush to my face
I coy away from you purposely
as you gently pull me close to your chest
you revealed a passion, in your madness
a dominance hidden, behind your touch
As your fingers interlock, playfully with mine
a love I could feel, you were ready to let go of

My love for you

I never asked
you never gave
My silent words
you could never hear
I felt your touch
I read your eyes
fulfilling every wish

Touch

Your touch always bought
the feeling of my first night
You caressed a part of my soul
that craves for your attention
and your eyes.

A dream

Sitting in a café
our morning tea and cakes
You in your spectacles
me with grey hair

Long distance

We drifted away from each other
forcefully pulled apart
We could only talk with our eyes
as our gaze held us together
I couldn't blame you for leaving
for the way things had ended
I never had the courage to stop you
or give you a reason to stay
Our moments we shared with one another
we packed and took away with us
to feel them in our seclusion
completely away from everyone
The burdens placed upon us
shaped the direction we swayed
torn apart by pressures and headaches
but your love they couldn't erase
I desired to see your face
and yearned to hear your voice
I begged to be heard, for the last time
enough to give me a purpose

The star we saw

The star we saw together
witnessed our oath of love
It gazes through my window
waiting for you to come

A memory

In the nights, when we would sneak out on a spree
drinking pink crème of cardamom saffron tea
You flirtatiously, take a sip from me
sharing the taste, from the same place of my lips
Holding me close, as the breeze touches my face
My resistance you felt, as you comfortably set it free
As we walk on the sand, warm bare feet
you trace my hair, a memory bitter and sweet

A part of me still wants you

I tried to remove your memories
from each box of my mind
Every time I sat on the prayer mat
my heart kept calling you back

A balm to my wounds

Your touch was a balm
to my open wounds
No matter how much I tried
it was only you that could heal

Intoxicate

Fumes of smoke, I inhale as I walk by
hit me in the face, as they slowly float high
Shisha, vapes, cigarettes they all light a flame
finding ways to ease, temporarily intoxicate
We soak our emotions, with toxins and liquids
lose the will to feel, to hear our own voices
We choose to numb our thoughts,
afraid to heal on our own
Why don't we trust ourselves

I still think of you

I sit imprisoned inside my heart
scribbling, sketching images and letters
on the walls of my conscious
Waiting to be set free

I wonder

I wonder if I was ever anything to you
A garment of each other, in the feelings we grew
It was easy for you to express so openly
I held each word back, listening carefully
You knew how I felt, with just one look in my eyes
You gave me the confidence, to speak up from inside
Why didn't you hold on, when my eyes asked you to stay
you left me with your pain
but you didn't tell me how to heal

Escapism

We all find ways to escape or hide
from watching a movie to reading a book
We look for images, that remind us of ourselves
a feeling we can relate to, words that ease our hearts
We're all holding onto something, we hear or see
a never ending battle, between you and me

Conscious and subconscious

My conscious
has let go of every part of you
But subconsciously
I still hold on to you

Words

The words beneath my skin
are invaluable pearls of wisdom
Not everyone can feel
or recognise them
The only gems
that saved my soul

Voice

I was deaf
to the voices
around me
the only voice
I could hear
was yours

Lost heart

It's okay to allow your heart
to wander sometimes
Seeing oneself frivolous
will always bring you back

I wish I could fly away

I wish I could fly, high up the skies
like the kites in your country, free from the ground
Fly over the seas and reach for the stars
away from the sorrows, away from my heart
If only I could feel, the air touch my soul
see the world from a distance, as I drift afar from it all

Time

Walking in this race of life
blind and lost
As time and age ticks away
you end up holding on to nothing
but your thoughts

A matter of dignity

My hands were tied, my mouth was sealed
A feeling of defeat, as my heart bled your name
accepting him was a matter of dignity
You became a name, I could only whisper
nurturing and preserving, your memories
in the museum, I built within me
I kept you alive, a part of me
You may have been forgotten
but for me, you still existed

Replaced

He came when I was melancholy
trying to heal through your memories
Whilst listening to the sound of my heartbeat
he was asking me to become a part of him

A relationship

An intertwined bond
a delicate cotton string
once detached
never the same

Years of Love

I lost myself, in the name of love
unaware of what I agreed, to become
My love oh sweetheart, was not of today
it was all those years I carried
since the very first day

Love

We grow up watching a melodrama, saga of eternal and undying love stories between two perfect icons. The romance and dialogues that blow us away, we eagerly wait until it's our turn. We create an imaginary definition of love, oblivious to the bitter truth that hides behind it all. The more we should run away from this idealism and stereotype of love, the more we are sucked into believing it exists.

When the pain of a heartbreak touches our soul, it's only then we realise what love actually is. The wounds they deliberately carve gradually becomes so deep that we become stubborn, not to go down the same road again. Still recovering from this burn not knowing how long it will take. We build our own realistic definition of love in our solitude. A love that closely resembles words that are egotistic and impermanent.

Love is not the sugar coated dialogues or the never ending rehearsed promises, but the silence behind it all. The touch that comforts your flaws, the eyes that honestly speak to you and the physical presence that protects you during every storm. It's as simple as that, but strangely very difficult to attain in this world.

With the passage of time you will see all the shades of love. Both conditional and unconditional love, eventually merge as one, until the difference becomes minute.

The only everlasting attachment that exists in the end, is the love between you and your spiritual self.

Spirituality is our greatest protection; from which we draw strength to persevere through hurdles in our lives. It helps us to understand and look beyond the material, to help us heal and repair in those moments, when love doesn't make sense at all.

Seven seas

I crossed the seven seas
only to be with you
You chose to come with me
looking for a place

I felt I found you

I felt I found you
but you came
to give new wounds
You were never mine

A promise unfulfilled

A kiss on the forehead
under the moonlight
a promise you could
never fulfil

Your words

Your words were music to my ears
touching each corner of my soul
your voice a familiar echo, even felt your absence
close and warm

The moon

In the nights, when you close the door
you go out to drink
my bitter coffee waits, for the taste you bring
I feel the loneliness, with the cup I hold
The moon from a distance, sits closer to me
silently listening, to each tear that falls

The moon, my companion
the only one that asks
are you happy my dear
you got what you desired
He talks in a language
showing things, I need to see
He tells me, he shines the brightest
in the nights when the sun sleeps
He loves to protect her, like he protects us all
prioritising his love over his needs

I tell him, hesitantly, I think I'm happy
I am healing, I'll compromise
but I see things, I never thought I would see

Blind faith

I never for a moment
doubted your intentions
or the possibility of a secret
you may have kept hidden all along
I trusted you more than
anyone else, I had ever known
My blind faith a reminder
of how foolish my heart was

My heart

I knew loving you was a risk
But I took this step
not to prove others
how right they were
But to prove my heart
its naivety can never lead

Your love was my foe

So quick to accept, whatever I showed
waiting until my heart, had been sewn with yours
Confused by your actions, contradicting your speech
It was only a matter of time, I saw your love as my foe
as you dug deeper, into my wounds as the years flowed

Under the stars

We both lay hand held under the stars
I made wishes for you
while you were lost in the thoughts
of something else

A lover or a liar

A liar artistically, disguised as a lover
fiercely fearless, beautifully rehearsed
It woes every corner, of your senses and nerves
leaving no room, for distrust or thoughts
Its touch paralyses, areas of spoken words
as they shrewdly prepare you, for your biggest fall

Not the man I loved

You can never return those years
my valuable time and energy
You gave nothing, but floods of tears
your false proclamations, affections of ease
I still kept you in my life
even when I realised, you weren't the one for me
Those wishes I made, to have you back
oblivious to the years, I missed in between

Promises

Your promise to never
leave, were just words
on the surface of your skin
The night you left
I will never forget
the way you made me feel

Unsteady hand

You steered the direction
of my path, with your
unsteady hand
A hand that only felt
firm in times of your
own carnal needs

Carry on

Love was one of many things
that taught me, you still carry on
walking even without your shoes

Struggle with real emotions

In this world full of concealed
emotions and people wearing masks
I suffer and struggle to carry my
real emotions without a mask

Your love fooled me twice

I loved you in a way, that your love taught me life
I gave you my loyalty, in return for your lies
The steps I took towards you
were wounded footprints of pride
When I asked you not to hurt me, you put your hand in mine
You tested me at every stage, as I quietly stood by your side
I took your pain, responsibilities, owning them as mine
When you asked what I had done for you
you were right to question why
You didn't see the sacrifices, I made for you sky high
I endured the pain you put me through
accepting it as one of my trials
The compromises I unwillingly made
you erased in the blink of an eye
When I asked if you would do the same for me
you turned your back behind

Illusion of love

The first time I saw you, I felt illusion
a whirlwind of butterflies, a feeling of fondness
A strange bond, I felt so deep
as you became a part of me
slowly taking me complete
Had I known, that this was all unreal
I wouldn't have slept
or even dared to dream

Presence and absence

Your presence
in my lighter moments
and absence
during my darker times
was all I needed
to make peace with my heart

Tough times

During my toughest time
wishing for those days to pass
I learnt to silence my heart
and listen to my brain

The other woman

I never thought I would lose you, to another woman
a woman, a wife, a part of your other life
Your overprotectiveness with the things back home
now makes sense to me, with the travels you made alone
Your ploy to come clean, after the birth of our child
I clap my hands in salute, for the script you conspired
I wanted to cry and laugh both hysterically
How you used my circumstances against me so articulately
Did you think I had become, insanely helpless
to accept her presence, alongside mine
You knew very well where I stood with you
even with the labels and pains, I carried because of you
We came so far with the efforts I devoted
The love we wanted to carry
was merely a feeling I ever wanted
I listened to the voice that always echoed
your name with honesty
What I felt for you, you slapped against my loyalty
Those voices of uncertainties
I regret pushing them away
One love was not enough for you
even when I gave you a share of my family
I screamed for you to stay
for all the sakes I could think of to say
You walked away from me
with an unfamiliar look in your eyes
as you silently watched me fall, to my feet
I forcibly looked into your eyes
your face I could no longer, recognise
I searched for my reflection, in anything I could find
but the answers all stood on her side

The truth

I thought letting you go completely
was going to be the most difficult
decision of my life
But you made it easier for me
by showing me who you really were

Hatred and pain

We have in our lives at some point felt hatred for someone so intense that it ends up hurting us more than them.

When someone really hurts us their sharp words and actions hit like arrows one after the other, as our hearts helplessly start to pulsate and breathe. Our minds suddenly switch off as we turn ourselves on defensive mode, where we lose the ability to say the right things and spit out all the wrong words. No matter how much we try and control ourselves in that moment, our souls begin to shiver in disbelief and anger as they light the match we've kept hidden.

It becomes our responsibility to keep the flame low throughout this period, which is very difficult to control. When the raging flame's reach higher and higher, we end up burning ourselves first. The strength of this destructive pain is such, that we end up carrying it for the rest of our lives.

We let our emotions of hatred and anger cry out either in our own space away from the object of our hatred, or by responding irrationally. .If we silence our words and reactions by distracting ourselves from our emotions, we are able to regain some control over our heart, mind and the vulnerability we feel during that time. This vulnerability which we forcefully control, portrays an image of strength and contentment to the person who hurt us, allowing us to step away from the situation rationally.

It is this hatred and pain that teaches us patience, discipline and resilience with our words and situations. If we can succeed in passing through this maze, we realise that hate is ephemeral. This hatred eventually turns into a puff of smoke, which gently leaves our bodies, no longer effecting us anymore.

Love not for me

I should have known the path of love
is forbidden for me to walk on
I don't know why I took a step towards you
again, knowing it wouldn't last for long

Pain relief

There was once a time
when I held you back
from smoking fumes
of slow misery
The same puff of insobriety
is now a pain relief for me

Courage

And so *you* gave me the
courage to let *you* go

9 months

Growing inside a seed of hope
My patience entangled
with all the pains I had to cope
As months pass by, I feel your little hicks
you tell me every day, you can hear me
through your subtle kicks
You feel my voice, you feel my touch
a guest I impatiently wait for
to hold my hand secure

Flowers

Flowers come handy
place them on your tombstone
gift them when you're born

Divorce

The cuts and bruises I hide underneath
Invisible to the body, but visible in my speech
You ask me my status, I reply I am divorced
You frown in bewilderment, a sense of compassion
an expression, an answer, I'm not looking for
My dried up tears, no longer cry anymore
As I'm numb to the tag, I wear all day long
It keeps me grounded, going upright strong
A taboo, a stigma, of the word we all fearfully run from
Happy to accept an open wound, but not the word divorce
The pressures of cultured societies, we silently bare it all
it doesn't matter what happens, behind closed doors
just don't bring the shame, the mess of the relation outdoors
What will people think, what will people say
let's just hide it all away, the dirt under the floor

Father

I'm sorry you'll grow up without your father
A father one day I felt will be your shadow
Your back bone, your strength, a man you could honour
The missing piece of your life, I'll step up for you and cover
I'm sorry I wasn't able, to choose the right partner
The mistakes I made unknowingly, you will have to suffer
I am glad your all mine
sorrows you won't have to share with another
I promise to hold you tight
until his absence no longer matters

Lost it all

I wish I had only
loved you from a far
than to bring you close
and lose it all

Your little face

You touch my face with your soft little hands
your big beady eyes expressive and profound
You remind me of the man, once a part of me
who left his silhouette engraved in your face

Your name doesn't sting

Your name lingers the smell, of an unforgotten scent
unable to wash off, as it lives within my veins
As I write my cognomen, my pen comes to a stop
taking a pause for breath, as I quickly scribble it across
I speak to spell my name, your presence a prompt again
Images of your memories blur, as I've finally accepted
it's just a name

Heavy heart

When the heart feels heavy
let yourself go
Let your emotions, pour over
those boundaries of control
The floods of pure water
only wash away the weight of your pain
For all those years
you soundlessly bravely carried

A poet

Your pain made me spiritual
your falsity bemused me
The restlessness I carried
poured on the page as poetry

A lover now a stranger

There was once a time
when you would wait outside
for a text to tell you, I'm home
My existence near or far, wherever I am
no longer means anything to you

Restless vs peaceful nights

I slept many restless nights
thinking about you, from dusk til dawn
You stole my amity and dreams
lost in the thoughts of remembering us
remembering you, knowing
we will be together one day

I sleep peacefully in the silent nights
silencing my thoughts with new dreams
awakened, with no more us,
no more you, putting my conscious
eternally at rest

Hardship

When a difficult time befalls us, it comes without any pre warnings. Our life could be as smooth as the ocean, with only seconds until the same water turns into vigorous waves. They wash us away from side to side as we struggle to breathe from underneath. We become tired and exhausted as we fight our way through, until our tears and the ocean become one entity.

Disorientated and filled with confusion, we hesitantly look for refuge and help with empty hands. We watch ourselves become helpless and hopeless, forgetting our true self-worth. This weakness and bitter truth, rips a part of our soul and pride; something we never forget as it remains with us like a permanent and unfading scar.

Our existence we come to know, is nothing but part of the same soil that we step on beneath our feet. Our character is tested in such a way, that we are able to see ourselves independent from the things and people that kept us secure and brought us comfort. What remains with us in the end is simply our own presence and shadow, comforting our solitude in our hardship.

Broken pieces

I learnt to recreate myself
from the mess, you left behind
Now when I stumble
across your pieces, it no longer
hurts or affects me
anymore

Well being

I spent my lost
precious days and time
on a relationship, so temporary
Ignorant to my everlasting
relationship, with my spiritual
wellbeing

Blessings change

When you're taken away from a blessing
it's always replaced with another
Your blurry eyes only become clear
when you're willing to focus on yourself
and in your circle, without fear

Mindfulness

My mindfulness
every so often teaches me
to taste the bitterness
of my own reality
with a drop of honey

I love you my child

I watch you from a distance, run faster in pace
with the little steps you take, owning your space
slow down I think, as I run behind you
afraid of the falls, that will soon follow you
You wonder carefree, with no thought or worry
a life so beautiful, as you have no story
Holding you close, as you speak to me
your eyes and smile, light the happiness I need
You babble words, that I can truly feel
only I will ever know, what you really say to me
My bundle of joy, my reason to live
promise me when you grow up
you won't forget who I am

Healed by motherhood

I feed you lovingly, a part of my skin
your head peeks out, as you catch my glimpse
I watch you suckle, softly and gently
forgetting for a moment, what it felt to feel happy
My tummy all crinkly, my half-moon scar
a reminder of my transition, from a woman to a Ma
Afraid to look in the mirror, with the changes outside
makes me wonder, there's nothing closer
to a mothers selfless love

I may have suffered, but it was worth it in the end
My boys give me no time, to fall apart or mourn
You left your absence, at the time when he needed you
I won this battle, by freeing myself, finally from you
My unrequited love, my son has gifted me
with a purity and affection felt so deep
expressed like no other, you will never feel

A mother is never alone

As I wake to the sounds of my two playful boys
opening, closing, going through my drawers
I see the little blessings, run around me explore
Why did I ever think I was alone
I hear fussy requests, of foods to eat
see the joy on their faces, when I sit down to feed
I watch them play, with their cars and toys
the happiness and laughter, together they show
I pick them up to cuddle and kiss
feel their comfort and love, they continuously give
holding me skin tight, small hands felt safe
every day I watch them, grow and grow
As I put them to bed, gently tucked away
I hear a small voice, asking me to stay
a feeling of wholeness, a feeling of bliss
Why did I ever think I would end up alone

Happiness

There comes a time when we take life too seriously with the baggage of responsibilities and the lessons taught by others. The true warmth of experiencing happiness within us, is lost somewhere far behind. The happiness we search for doesn't touch our hearts in the way it used to, that it now almost frightens us when we somehow even come close to the feeling. We have conditioned ourselves to laugh from the surface of our hearts, which instantly fades as soon as the moment comes to an end

Our hearts that were once filled with purity and innocence, is now contaminated by the sins of others, with toxins of pain, negativity and emotions that we've taken upon our self to swim and agonise in. We should only take accountability to try and clean up the water step by step at a time, through patience and positivity. Looking for the smaller things in our lives that bring back our lasting smiles and happiness.

Loving yourself is still possible

I never knew I could love myself
more than I loved you
Until I saw you love yourself more
than you ever loved me

Finding myself

The grief and heartache
you put me through
gave me the wisdom
to search within myself
Being able to realise who I am
is far greater than the value
of losing you

Three words only

I was able to save myself
from you, because I
knew the value of those
three words

Peace in prayer

I used to find comfort
in your sweet deception
Now I've learnt to find it
in the purity above
as my forehead simply
touches the ground

Prayer

The sound of the call
your remorse brings you close
as your overflowing heart
drops in tears to the floor
With the books on your shoulders
and nothing in your hands
the ache that you carry
we plead to bury
beneath the soil

Faith in yourself

We often become too dependent on others, that we begin to doubt our own capability and life without them. We can hate others for leaving us at the wrong time in our lives. But when we eventually learn to detach ourselves from this pain, we are able to understand and see clearly that their absence was actually better for us, and in many ways a blessing.

Wherever our present now comfortably sits, is because of the hurt we endured. Behind this pain is the key to unlocking our abilities and confidence to allow us to step closer to our success and independence.

We only need to take the first step of simply believing in ourselves just a little, which is enough for us to go a long way.

Freedom

I have finally found my freedom
after many years of fight
free from the burdens, my heart and mind
achingly carried inside
Is it late or a blessing, that I missed
the rebellion time
my principles, values and morals
have now already been defined
Have I truly found freedom
to be my only self
attached to me and liabilities
are the things that hold me back

Time

When we look back counting our years by progress, success or material profit; we feel proud and self-assured that we utilised our time well. It would seem illogical to most if I said that those years could be measured as our wasted time.

We forget that every day we have lived and continue to live, we make a conscious decision of what we are doing, who we are meeting and where we travel in our busy lives.

When everything seems to fall nicely in place, we become even less conscious, we don't question our time or pause to think. We just continue at our pace until we hit a brick wall abruptly coming to a stop.

When we experience a failure or loss, it's during this period that time teaches us its value. We allow ourselves to step back from the world, thinking much deeper about our relationship with time and the connection we have with this world.

Our mind starts to question our contentment, existence, in explainable thoughts, our place and our true relations. Most importantly we question our purpose in this world as we start to grow our inner maturity and explore our spirituality. This period of time we often feel is wasted when actually it is the only real time we truly begin to understand and save ourselves from the illusions of love, success and happiness that the world has created for us to live in.

Love or hate

Should I hate you
for the lesson you taught
or thank you for the pen
you placed between my fingers

Mistakes set me free

My life was nothing, but a sequence of mistakes
one after the other, each fall deeper than before
Mistakes I intensely analysed, never to repeat again
as I have no room for you, or anyone anymore
the amusing part was, they all knew how bad you were
and I still waited to see you, destroy the person I was
In this pursuit of pleasing others and cherishing hurt
I left my soul in agony, of the years it borne
tainted, broken, but a new version for the world to see

Definitions

When I look back at myself
the eyes once new to the world
My words and their meanings
pure as gold
now changes colour daily

Mother and a maid

During the day, I'm a mother and a maid
I forget who I am, as I pull the weight
The dishes pile up, singing high and tall
I hoover the carpet, picking crumbs off the floor
The kids scream about shouting, someone's at the door
Taking letters from a man, a name I never know
Polishing and laundry, as I turn the volume down
The kids start yelling, we want some food right now
Breakfast, lunch and dinner is served
Moving to the dishes, that were kept reserved
Scrubbing and cleaning, rooms top to bottom
Already time for snack and his seven ounce bottle
Clearing up the mess, from what they leave behind
I finish off the leftovers, food I hate to waste
thinking to myself, will I ever get some rest

As the day comes to an end
I make a strong cup of tea
A cup I've learnt to make for myself
as there's no one else to make for me
held tight and sipped slow
the only feeling, that never leaves
As I catch a moment to myself
finally being away from the sailing sea

A loyal star

As I look up in the sky
I see a star shining bright
Stood neatly in the flawless sheet
proudly silent high
Alone it makes its appearance
for the world to look up in awe
It speaks to us in a way, lost with our words
So caught up in this selfish world
the stars make time for us
They glow for each and everyone
that wander confused and alone
They come out to tell us
that we are not on our own
Worlds apart from them
but they watch and listen to us all
We can never question their loyalty
their existence in our lives
they never change their colours
or their paths in the way they arrive

The sky

Ever wonder if we are the only creation to feel the whirlpool of emotions that the world throws at us. It's easy for us to show what we feel, as we let our emotions manifest through our facial expressions, behaviours and words.

Looking up in the sky we see a ray of colours and moods; a mirror of our own projections.

One look at the sky leaves us astounded with the mixture of messages we feel and interpret. The family that makes up the entire galaxy comes out during different days and times. We find images and faces in the slow moving clouds, personalised for each one of us to see what we need to. The sky like us changes colour with its aura. We feel its impulsive emotions every day, every month, every year. It cries out pouring rain and in anger or love covers the sky in shades of passionate reds. It feels the pain we feel after every drop of water and creates a rainbow of magic showing us that after each dull moment, happiness and hope gradually makes its way.

The sky itself is an inspiration for us, as we unknowingly share a deep relationship with it. When the sun shines on us we forget our pain and troubles. We watch the beautiful sunset comfort our eyes and soul. The nights provide us shelter with a dark blanket. It watches us switch off, our souls departing our shell. The stars and the moon come out to speak; companions for the lonely souls struggling to sleep.

The sky and its family walking alongside us every step. Pain or pleasure, grief or glory, cannot shrug off the sun and moon following behind and witnessing it all.

The moon follows me

Driving home, my son brings a smile
as he asks me why is the moon following me
Everywhere I go, I hide from it
but it always finds me

Solitude

When your solitude
learns to comfort
your silent chaos
you'll never find ways
to escape from it

My only reason why

I pick up the pieces, of strength and courage
A mother, woman and a wounded soul
Every day I seek to be closer
finding relief in your beads and blessings
The pain of those difficult roads
remind me of who I have become
A person I never thought I could be
Alone in this battle, with you in my heart
you guide me spiritually, through my prayers
your signs making ways, I eventually see
For you are the only one, who knows how I feel
To you we all return to, with your name only
my journey continues

I watch the world go by

I sit by the balcony, watch the world go by
the busy roads, the tall buildings glowing in the night
I can feel the cold breeze deep within my soul
a feeling I longed for, letting myself go
As I look around me, a race amongst time
of everything, we think we need
A place made of travellers, relations we make weak
Imbedded inside us, are gardens of flowers
unsure whether to water, we just let them wilt in silence
A fulfilment of the soul, we are never able to feed
in the end we watch ourselves, slowly covered in leaves

Reminisce

And sometimes all I can do
is visit myself
in places I once were
without you
and without the pain
of those people
a part of this world

The things we chase

The object, commodity or element
we centralise and focus, our entire lives over
is the very same thing, that will end up
being your biggest trial
Hurting you the most, as it leaves

Forget me not

You may not think of me now
but one day you will
You'll see a part of me somewhere
 hidden beneath
A place, a building
A person, a name
A glimpse, a painless blur
that will strangely pull you back
As the wind whispers my name
deep into your soul
you will hear your conscious speak to me
at a time, when your far too late

My journey

In this journey of loving you
finding you to lose you
I fell, to be able to walk
to walk long enough, to run

My wellbeing
my heart and soul
are the only things
that will protect me
from everything
you couldn't do

Lines on your hands

The lines on your hands
are written in pencil
how you define it with your pen
is all in your mind and control

Name fades

I revisit those places
we once made memories
As I subconsciously search you
your son wipes them away

Single motherhood

When I became a single mother, it was one of the most toughest and painful realities of my life. It was during this period I learnt the intensity a woman could compromise and sacrifice herself, for the sake of providing her children the life she had always imagined; despite her own trials.

I have felt motherhood very differently, that it changed my 'motherly' experience and pain into a lesson of wisdom and growth, as I slowly watched my vulnerability flourish into strength.

My patience and ability to take on and cope with the pressures of responsibilities, that I without choice was thrown into, tested my self-belief, emotions, pains, insecurities and anxieties of not only being a mother but a father and myself, all at the same time.

When I thought that my world had all fallen apart, I was continually reminded at every step that followed how wrong I really was.

It took some time for me to come out of my feeling of bereavement. I let my emotions pour out for as long as I needed them to, for me to accept what had happened.

I felt depressed and ashamed that because of my misjudgements and choices, my children would have to suffer the consequences. I could barely look after myself from the trauma I had experienced, and the thought of raising my children on my own, seemed all too daunting and impossible for me to do.

There were times where I craved to be left alone in solitude, holding on to the words and prayers of my faith. I realised that I had nothing else and no one to confide in, other than Allah who was putting me through this trial.

Feeling lost and bemused, I silently swept along with time until I occupied myself in chores, gradually falling into a new routine. Over time I came to terms with my emotions and developed a rational approach to dealing with my heart and mind.

My mind which was strong and firm spoke of time, endurance and acceptance. My heart was weak, soaked in emotions and gave me false hopes, empathy and feelings of desperation.

My conscience and desire for self-respect, didn't allow me to accept what my heart was saying to me anymore. It wanted me to feel inferior and vulnerable again like I had already. I needed to be strong and resilient for my children, as it wasn't just about me anymore.

As I started to feed my mind with positivity and take a pragmatic approach, the direction of my life started taking shape. My focus diverted solely to my children as their needs became my priority. I was gradually able to learn that I could switch my roles of when I needed to be a mother and when to be a father. I slowly started to push my grieving-self back, as I unknowingly left her far behind.

My health was deteriorating as I started to lose more weight. I was continuously fighting a battle from within. When I looked at my children who were only dependent on me, it was unfair and hurtful to see that of no fault of theirs, they were being affected because of me. It was then I picked up the courage to change myself completely, and focused my life on maintaining my financial, mental and physical strength and stability.

My financial struggles allowed me to see the true colours of the so-called claimants of 'love' and 'care'. The ones who understood my silence were always there by my side. The ones who stepped away; their faces engraved deep down into my soul.

Growing up being taught that the hand that gives is always better than the hand that receives, bled me further knowing that in just a split of a second, I had come to the other side of that hand. It shattered my pride, ego and confidence which made me become stubborn and angry as I decided to maintain silence.

I didn't seek for any help or support from my family, who were unable to recognise the struggles I was going through. Meticulous budgeting, saving and living within my means, was the only way I was able to face myself and my children.

As my financial liabilities grew, I quietly struggled mentally and physically. I hid my feelings, pressures and burdens, ensuring my children and my family were oblivious to what I was going through.

My pain didn't completely vanish, but it started to fade as my sorrows were slowly being replaced by the happiness my boys were bringing me every day.

With time my children became my source of healing, as they showed me how much they needed and loved me. Their cries for my attention and their eyes that would search for me in my absence nurtured a new type of love I had never felt. The affection and wholeness I found myself empty of, was now being filled by the unconditional love of my two boys. The attachment that grew between us, assured me they were truly a part of me. They were the only ones that saved me from what could have been my self-destruction.

Motherhood for me is not the pain of birth or the sleepless nights. It is a journey that allowed me to find my identity as an independent and complete woman. Being a mother taught me that women are well capable of filling the shoes of an absent father, persevering despite their own pain. They can live up to and provide at every level the need, desire, wants and emotional attachments of their children, ensuring that nothing is left incomplete in their lives.

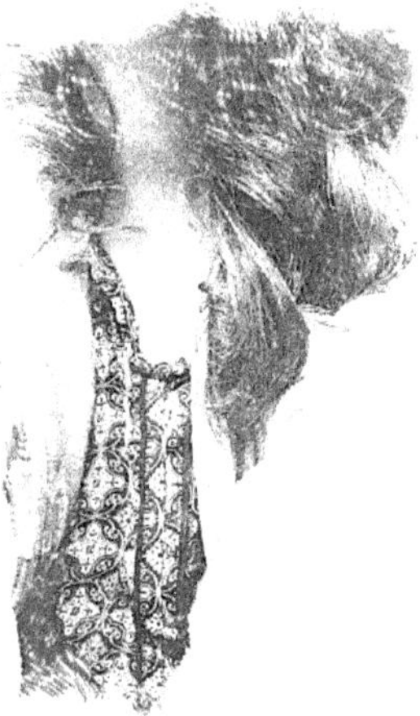

The scars of life

I ask myself what have I achieved in a world,
where success is seen and admired
I count the scars, that I have gained along the way
The scar from the one I loved, showed me how to see
the lies behind your words
truth in their actions, we often forget to see
The scars from those I trusted, shaped me to be
my own saviour, a shield for my children
the independent person that I am today
The scars that remind me of my pain,
allow me to see, how far I have travelled
My scars of mistakes, have turned into tattoos
Tattoos that live to tell a story, deep inside, a part of me

You ask what have I achieved in a world,
where success is seen and admired
The will, strength and patience
to endure and fight it all

Modesty in words

In the world we live today
the word modesty is fading away
We cover less, speaking
recklessly everywhere
The way we wear ourselves
we become unaware of our
inner and reflective self
So liberated in our actions
we don't care about
other people's reactions
Liberation of the mind
doesn't mean you speak
completely blind
Learn the value of words
speak less as our tongue
is no less of a sword
Our soul and words
define our existence
think how we represent
and scent our essence.

Stages of life

The day you are born, you open your eyes
The only years of life, you see faces of innocence
As you grow older, hit your teenage years
your mum and dad, begin to pull you near
Don't do this, don't do that
you know nothing, about the wolves outside
You roll your eyes, feeling helpless and lost
taking a stroll down the road
waiting for something to drop

You reach your adult years, you either marry or find a career
obscure in the journey, of finding your purpose
It's only a matter of time, before your moulded, defined
by your parents, or by the shadow of others
You count your deeds, walking very carefully
as karma can come round, unexpectedly
You face your fears, until life brings you to tears
still in the search, of your destination
Culture, values and materialistic covers
chained around your neck, new burdens you carry
Forced to see the world, through your new set of lens
limitations placed on our souls, and on our steps
The pressures of relations, society and rules
you strap on you wrist, as you continue to move
When you feel the breaking point
you question purpose, beliefs and goals
settled, wanderer or lost

You reach your old age, where everything feels late
tired, waiting, dependant but wise
You hold your chain and strap with all the pain and lessons
taking them gracefully with you to the grave

I could never be the person
that I was before I met you

My old self was never adept
for the journey fate had chosen
for me to walk on